Runaway with Words:

A Collection of Poems
from Florida's Youth Shelters

Edited and Introduced by Joann Gardner
Director, Runaway with Words

Anhinga Press 1997
Tallahassee, Florida

Cover art: *Self Portrait* by Alfred Simmons
Cover design by Tina Bromberg and Jennie Malcolm
Book design and production by Lynne Knight

Library of Congress Cataloging-in-publication Data:

Runaway with Words: A collection of Poems from Florida's Youth Shelters / edited and introduced by Joann Gardner. — 1st edition

ISBN 0-938078-47-X
Library of Congress Cataloging Card Number 96-079886

Anhinga Press Inc. is a nonprofit corporation dedicated wholly to the publication and appreciation of fine poetry.
For personal orders, catalogues and information, write to:
Anhinga Press, P.O. Box 10595, Tallahassee, FL 32302.

Printed in the United States of America
First Edition, 1997

Contents

IV. Letters and Conversations

V. Pictures and Words

VI. Body Talk

VII. Animals and Totems

VIII. Heroes

IX. The Numbers Game

X. Hopes, Dreams, and Fears

XI. Love

XII. Laughter

Index

Acknowledgements

I would like to thank Janet Heller, whose idea it was to bring poetry into Florida's youth shelters and who, in conjunction with the Florida Network of Youth and Family Services, founded Runaway with Words. Janet taught with me for the first two years of the program and helped collect many of the poems that would come to be included in this anthology.

I would also like to thank the staff of the Florida Network for their support of Runaway with Words, specifically Christopher Card, the former Executive Director, and Richard Nedelkoff, the current Executive Director, who have incorporated Runaway with Words into their services to shelters and have kept important promises. Also, many thanks to Network staff members Angie Allen and JoAnn Harrell who generously applied themselves to various Runaway with Words duties: Angie, who assisted with grant writing and other administrative activities associated with the program, and JoAnn, who put together handsome promotional materials. I am also grateful to Fred Sanguiliano, former Director of Training and Evaluation at the Network, for providing crucial information in a pinch.

Thanks, too, to the sites we have visited over the past five years and to the participating staff members of: Hidle House (Panama City); Interface (Gainesville); Sarasota YMCA; Family Services Program (Orlando); PACE Center for Girls (Jacksonville, Orlando, Tallahassee); Miami Bridge Central and Miami Bridge Homestead (Miami); Haven Poe Runaway Center (Tampa); BEACH House (Daytona Beach); Arnette House (Ocala); Youth Crisis Center, North and South (Jacksonville); Youth and Family Connection (St. Petersburg and Clearwater); Capital City Youth Services (Tallahassee); YouthBuild (Tallahassee). The individuals associated with these programs invited us into their space, gave freely of their time, and helped us generate exciting work.

Runaway with Words would not have been able to develop without the dedication and skill of Florida State University graduate students. I would, thus, like to thank Sandra Gail Teichmann, the late Michael Gearhart (1957-1996), Jennifer von Ammon, and Janet Mauney for participating in the University Planning Grant project that helped us prepare for future teacher trainings. I would also like to thank the students in my service-learning courses: first,

Amy Cashulette Flagg, Doug Ford, Dorinda Fox, Kitty Gretsch, Stephanie Harrell, Genyne Henry, and Cadence Kidwell, who took "Writing with the At-Risk Population" and responded well to the challenge of newness; then, Kammi Berry, Jarred Bistrong, James Bowers, Debbie Hall, Patricia Hendricks, Andre Lawrence, Sarah Royalty, Rachel Sutz, and Betty Tartar, who invested their energy and intelligence in the "Writing as Outreach" course. All of these students contributed much more in the way of time, patience, and attention to their work than can adequately be reflected by any grade.

I am grateful as well to The Department of English at Florida State University, specifically to Karen Laughlin (Assistant Chair) and to Anne Rowe (Chair), whose moral support and administrative good sense have made up for a host of difficulties, and to English Instructor Pat MacEnulty, who, for 1995-96, took care of the program's loose ends. I miss Jerry Stern, who, when I saw him in the halls at FSU would always inquire after the program. I would thank him if I could for his long-term friendship and support.

I am indebted as well to Anhinga Press and its board members for recognizing the importance of this project and for seeing it through to publication: to Director Rick Campbell, whose wise counsel, patience, and sense of humor never let the setbacks set him back; to Lynne Knight whose care and attention to type set and design framed the poems and introductions elegantly; to Stephanie Sgouros whose proofreading skills helped eliminate textual errors; to Geoff Brock who prepared promotional materials; to Van Brock whose experience teaching children and publishing their poetry provided an important precedent, and to Hank Osborne for his fundraising efforts and ideas.

I would also like to thank my friend Tina Bromberg, alias Cadie Jones, who worked on the cover design and provided essential encouragement during hard times, and Jennie Malcolm, who contributed her time to cover fonts and layout. It is heartening to have such friends, to be able to depend on their quiet artistry and intelligence.

Various agencies have provided funding for Runaway with Words projects over the years. In this regard, The Florida Arts Council deserves recognition, as do Winn Dixie Family Charities, AT&T, and the FSU Foundation. Without their help, we could not have printed workbooks, bought supplies, trained teachers, offered workshops, or prepared numerous performances and presentations to share with the public.

Finally, I would like to thank the kids, for what they have given me and what they have given themselves in the way of hope and achievement, especially Alfred, Frantz, Star, Beverly, Sylvia, Mevonda. . . and others I have met, who have impressed me with their strength and goodness and have made this work especially rewarding and necessary.

Introduction

I. Precedent

In his introduction to *A Spot of Purple is Deaf*, Anhinga Press's first collection of children's poetry published in 1974,[1] Van K. Brock spoke of the ease with which children connect the inner self with the outside world. Poetry is freedom of thought, Brock claimed, and conventional —"bad" or "false"— education thwarts creativity by imposing expectations of correctness on expression. "Children poets," he tells us, "have in common with the better adult poets a love for vigorous expressive language and surprising reversals of expectations."

What is crucial about Brock's statement, aside from its specific insight, is that it needed to be said at all. Even in the movement-oriented climate of the 1970s, the publication (reading or study) of children's work required some justification. In approaching his subject aesthetically, rather than practically or emotionally, Brock addressed the cultural prejudices of his adult audience. Writing by children negotiated a wide spectrum of imaginative possibilities, with a naturalness and simplicity unavailable to self-censoring adults. It deserved our attention not only because it took us where we could not go ourselves but it suggested ways of energizing and renewing poetry.

Twenty-three years later, the issue for this anthology is still one of validation: how do poems written by children affect us, or, more pointedly, how do poems by "at-risk" children impact on our idea of art? The argument of innocence is not possible in this case, since participants in the Runaway with Words program — all clients of one of the Florida Network's 22 member agencies[2] — have had sufficient life-experience to be downright jaded, but the argument for uniqueness — that these young writers have perspectives and skills that are beyond us in some way — remains potent.

While lawmakers ponder how best to invest their dollars, while parents try to deal effectively with their children's behavior, while child advocates speak eloquently for or about them, their own voices are blocked by their inability or unwillingness to speak for themselves. Bringing these young people to the table, offering them opportunities and skills in self-expression not only provides them with some control over their own lives but opens up a whole new dimension of creative endeavor, one in which verbal simplicity and experience combine to produce a unique and profoundly affecting art.

The bridge between the academy and the street is difficult to make, yet the scholar, the academician, the poet all gain for having done so. In adapting my own writing to the shelter situation, I have developed new perspectives and skills: a growing ability to write under pressure, a commitment to engaging important social issues, a sense of how to proceed naturally without strident argument or cant. Having ventured this far across the rhetorical boundary, I will offer an example:

I remember meeting at my first workshop in Panama City a gangly 14-year-old named Moses. Moses had no claims to literary excellence, but he did have more than the usual dose of defiant wit. When asked to write a poem about a part of his body that would help us understand him, Moses wrote about his penis. The poem was calculated to shock, with its claims about the size and responsiveness of Moses's penis, its willingness to get him into trouble, but somewhere in the middle of this exposé, Moses got lost. He forgot about his own excellence and began to focus on the real object of his expression, a girl with beautiful red hair. The shock of discovery came in the tenderness of the last line, a perception of the girl so clear and honest that everyone knew how Moses felt.

Despite the intended defiance of this composition, the disposable sense of style, Moses's poem was successful the way the best poems are successful. It lingered in the mind, inviting us back to it for the pleasures we might find there. I cannot quote from it the way I would have done had it belonged to a recognized literary tradition or had I had the foresight or the ability to save it (Moses himself dismissed our praises and tucked it away in his workbook), but when I consider why its loss may have been significant, I suspect it has something to do with what it could have shown us — about personality, about universality, about surprising reversals of expectations.

Moses began his poem as a joke, a series of off-color allusions meant to embarrass his audience and make his teacher reconsider her job, but he ended in a moment of high seriousness, having discovered the truth of his own desire and the vulnerability of his own caring. This is sophisticated knowledge, and the turn the poem made, the shift in attitude and awareness, offered the same cathartic reward that writers have always sought and commonly identify with success. Perhaps, too, the reward was enhanced in this case, because the poem came from a writer from whom not much was expected. In a simple expression, Moses helped us understand his own experience of puberty and the complicated emotions that accompanied it.

My desire for Moses' poem over the past five years offers the best argument I can muster for anthologies of this kind. I may have assumed that other, equally outrageous expressions would appear to take its place. I may have thought that it played no essential role in the program's history or the evolution of a culture still to be expressed. But, in its tone, approach, style, voice, and moment, it had captured the pleasure and intimacy of that first workshop. It was Moses' own contribution, and there was no replacing it with something else. There was only admitting that we had lost it and determining, as best we could, that we would not let other expressions disappear as well.

Many such poems have been hidden under mattresses, folded into workbooks, or thrown away, because the author did not believe in them, because others did not demonstrate sufficient interest; but collections of this kind reflect the challenges of its contributors (those they face as well as those they issue for us), and they demonstrate how verbal simplicity may be used to expressive advantage. The imagination is an important resource. It provides a means by which the unapproachable may be examined and resolved, and it reaches across boundaries of age, distance, time, and class to communicate crucial messages. One way to evaluate such expressions, to assess their place in our culture, is to read and respond to them the way we would any composition, poem, piece of art that provokes thought or communicates feeling. If we are moved by an expression, if it changes or captivates us, how can we dismiss it from importance, even though it is written by a child?

II. The Program
Runaway with Words is a poetry workshop for at-risk youths. Founded in 1991 by Janet Heller and myself, it works with the belief that creative self-expression has therapeutic value, helping in-

dividuals confront difficult emotional issues and increasing self-esteem. Each series of workshops has a clearly defined goal. Students, teachers, and on-site staff cooperate to produce poems that will be shared with others, in the form of performances, publications, or exhibits of the program's work. Knowing that their writing will reach audiences outside the shelter environment encourages participants' best efforts, and many have achieved far more in the way of compelling writing than was ever expected or imagined of them.

When Janet and I first visited the shelters, we had only limited experience with at-risk teens. Janet herself had had a difficult adolescence, and she had worked for a year as a teacher in a rural community outside of New Orleans. I had substitute-taught special education students at a high school in Maine and had done some summer teaching in "Operation Summer Help," but the better part of my adult life had been spent working at a university with students who are generally older and more blessed than those of the shelter environment. Fortunately, we had sufficient foresight to anticipate the challenges of this venture, and we went into it with a certain amount of humility and respect.

I was not convinced that my university teaching would translate well into this situation, and I felt that the subject matter, too, would have to be adjusted according to our expressed goal of therapy. But I had to begin somewhere, and it seemed only logical to begin with what I knew and then adapt it to what I could gain from direct experience. I, thus, brought with me six pages of cartoons and information on what I thought poetry was and how it should be done, but I remained open to the ideas and reactions of my audience. I was curious as to where they stood, whether poetry would have a life of its own and what it would look like in their hands. We discovered, almost immediately, that no one needed a definition of the word, that they all seemed to understand when asked to write "a poem about . . ." or "a poem that . . ." Some, it turned out, had written poetry on their own and had volumes of verse stashed away in their rooms; others wanted explanations, not so much of what it *was*, but what it was *for*. We responded as best we could to their questions, pointing out some of the ways writing had enhanced our lives. We helped them with technical and mechanical difficulties; they helped us with our own evolving sense of art.

As a result of this approach, both Janet and I encountered many shelter youth who wanted to share their expressions with us. They wanted to know if they "were any good." They wanted us to like and admire them. They appreciated the opportunity of working with "real writers" who could understand and validate their efforts. We enjoyed getting to know them, admired their strength, tried to wind our imaginations as tightly as theirs, and to produce work that would please and inspire them. While we had some "bad" moments in these workshops, we also had some very good moments that swept us up in pleasure, surprise, and, yes, fulfillment. Moses' penis poem was one such moment, as was Star's poem on incest, her generosity in sharing it with me and explaining its symbolism. I remember hearing her read it in front of a large audience at a Network conference and marvelling at how she had been transformed, through her writing, from a passive victim to an eloquent authority.

When, in 1994, graduate students began to train for and teach in the Runaway with Words program, I had to translate what I had learned into a set of guidelines for others. We discussed issues of cooperation and respect, and I told my prospective teachers that the best test of success would be the number and quality of poems collected at the end of the day. While some considered this precept too calculated, too restrictive, others saw it as a useful reminder of the program's situation and goals. If they had spent too much time being "teacher," if they had depended on "next time" for expressive breakthroughs, they were continually disappointed. They would return to the workshop the next week to discover that the class had shifted, the participants had moved on, and that they were faced with the prospect of starting again. Similarly, if they had launched into assignments without first establishing coherence or trust, then the students would not produce at all or they would only produce what was expected of them: mediocre work. Many graduate students were inspired by their experiences in the shelters, as I had been before them, and as the poems in this book demonstrate, we received a good number of "miracles" to suggest the participants' pleasure as well.

III. The Map
Runaway with Words workshops are organized in the shape of a circle, a metaphor for the democratic process that underlies

our methodology. Some sense of that shape is carried over into the anthology itself, where individual poems and sections complement each other, and various voices echo and play off each other. While the book itself is linear, one can begin reading anywhere without disrupting the sense of sequence. In other words, appreciation is cumulative rather than progressive the way a textbook or conventional narrative would be. Because the average stay of any child in the shelter is seven to ten days, workshops must be self-contained, and trust must be established quickly if it is to be established at all. Participants, thus, are given equal opportunity to contribute to the workshop, and, when they leave, they take with them important insights into some aspect of poetic craft — either in the Word, the Line, the Stanza, Image & Metaphor, or Music & Rhythm. Technical information is supplemented by exercises in the five senses, which sharpen the writer's sensual awareness and help ground the poem in real (felt) concerns.

The present publication celebrates the accomplishments and surprises that grew out of Runaway with Words workshops over the past five years. It provides an overview of the program, a sense of the off-beat, sometimes hysterical tone of these sessions, and it establishes a sense of permanence for an experience that is by nature fleeting. For some who have participated in Runaway with Words, it restores the pleasure of significant events. For others who have not, it represents the creative potential of the at-risk experience, its urgency and unpredictability. For all who work in the shelter environment, who understand the practical applications of art, it provides a valuable teaching tool.

This anthology is organized according to themes and exercises that promoted the best thoughts and expressions in our workshops. Each section is introduced with descriptive commentary, offering contextual information, anecdotes, and sample exercises relevant to the topic at hand. Contextual information provides an overview of some aspect of the shelter experience. Anecdotal evidence focuses on an individual associated with the program and a significant scene from the workshop. Sample exercises provide a writing assignment related to the focus of that chapter. In addition to presenting the work of shelter youth, I have included poems by staff, who put themselves in the position of apprentices and worked alongside their so-called clients. Staff writing has not been recognized or published in other places, even though it provides an essential foil for participants' work and demonstrates intrinsic value. It seems only fitting, thus, to include it in this overview. I did not include poems that I or other workshop leaders wrote because we have had (and do have) other opportunities for sharing our work.[3] The brief introductory prose pieces, however, present my own perspective on these encounters and offer some sense of what working in the shelters is like.

I have no doubt that on some level the poems in this book are political, where images and words speak, either directly or indirectly, for social change. I also believe that Runaway with Words is itself a political undertaking, providing an outlet for otherwise voiceless individuals in an ongoing social debate. Impersonal issues of policy and power ultimately depend upon simple, personal concerns — in this case, the right of everyone to be loved, to have security from which to grow, to have something or someone in which or whom to believe. The strategy of the powerful with respect to the powerless, often, is to ignore that which disturbs the status quo. In speaking out according to their own experience, these young people attest to problems in the world. They tell us the truth about who they are and what they would be, given the gift of security, love, and belief. Those of us who engage in and respect creativity see the hopefulness of such expressions, even when they are speaking of suffering and abuse.

In the past five years, I have learned a great deal from my students, both in and out of the at-risk environment. I have come to understand that young people need and respond to poems written in their own language, not just as verbal models or effective writing prompts, but as a means of connecting with and learning from others like themselves. I have discovered that readers and writers benefit from difference, that in extending oneself beyond the limits of daily experience, one rediscovers newness and possibility in writing. And I have found that partnerships between seemingly diverse groups can generate enormous creative energy, providing expressive foils for experience, values, choices, and methods of instruction. Interacting with these young people, familiarizing myself with their lives, I have gained a fresh approach to language and new perspectives on old themes. For me, poetry is a social act, and poets are enriched to the extent that they include others in their vision. By engaging in this exchange, we are defining who we are, where we come from, and what we hope to be.

In the past, Runaway with Words has put together chapbooks of student work, published individual pieces in the Runaway with Words workbook, the Florida Network newsletter, and its annual report.[4] We have not, with the exception of a few poems printed in our workbook, collected these expressions across boundaries of geography and time. From the beginning, we gathered poems from participants with the intention of anthologizing the best and the most representative works. We also saw this process as an effective way of keeping track of our activities, within each workshop and over time at various sites. It takes time to accumulate quality materials and to begin to see these materials as part of a coherent whole. Now that Runaway with Words has a history and an established methodology to draw from, it is easier to conceive of these separate events as part of an ongoing experience and to create from individual voices a harmony of song.

— Joann Gardner
Tallahassee, Florida
October, 1996

References

[1] *Lime Tree Prism* (1972) was the first anthology of the Poets in the Schools program. Profits from this collection helped fund *A Spot of Purple is Deaf*, the first collection to bear the Anhinga label. Van Brock and Francis Poole also collaborated on an anthology of prison poems, *The Space Behind the Clock* (1975), also published by Anhinga.

[2] The Florida Network of Youth and Family Services is an umbrella agency for some 22 youth shelters and alternative high schools. In addition to representing children's interests in state government, the Network compiles statistical information concerning client intake and placement, provides professional trainings for shelter staff, and sponsors Runaway with Words.

[3] *Back to Front*, a chapbook of poems by Joann Gardner and Janet Heller, Red Window Press (1993). Also, *Live Words; Live Words*, a medley of creative works and commentary from Runaway with Words workshops, performed by Runaway with Words teachers and writers, at the Warehouse, Tallahassee, 1995.

[4] See, for example, *Runaway wih Words: A Short Course on Poetry and How to Take it with You*, Joann Gardner, the Florida Network of Youth and Family Services (1996). Also, *The Network News* (1994) and *A Celebration of Service: 1995 Annual Report* (1995).

"There is no change without dream,
as there is no dream without hope."
— *Paulo Freire*

I. Street Life, Shelter Life

Contexts:

Most of us have only a limited sense of what it's like to be a runaway — why kids leave home, the challenges and hardships they encounter when they commit themselves to the streets. We become aware of them only when they interfere with our own lives: when they break the law, harm us physically, or pose a threat to our financial well-being. Then, we must work through our own anger to punish them before we can focus compassionately on their situation. The young people we have met in the shelters are not hopeless or depraved. They are, many of them, confused, angry, needy, and depressed, but they have found a way to be hopeful, or at least to carry on with their lives. What strikes us about these young people is their ultimate resiliency and humanity, in which we inevitably see something of ourselves, struggling under difficult circumstances to survive. They have responded favorably to the attention we have given them. They have suspected or feared that we would leave them, as everyone else has done, as we must do eventually. They have taught us about life on the street, life in the shelter, what it takes out of you, what it has to give.

Anecdotes:

Frantz was an 18-year-old African American male, articulate, courteous, and intelligent, whom we discovered one evening at a workshop at Miami Bridge. Unlike his peers, who had been brought to the shelter as a result of a judge's order, he had come here on his own, and, thus, considered the shelter a place of refuge, rather than the prison or holding tank the others were convinced it was. His hair was closely cropped on the sides, with a bloom of dreads emerging from the top — a self-styled "do" that advertised his individuality and self-approval. He treated his peers with respect and did not seem particularly rattled by the chaos that swirled around him. As others in the workshop grew distant, began to engage in hostile exchanges, pace, or leave the room, Frantz focused more intently on his writing. Huddled against a swirl of noise, he refused to let us go, and, when it came time for us to pack up and leave, he asked when we were coming back. The difficulty of this workshop, the seeming futility of our efforts here, and the psychological punishment we absorbed as a result of it, almost kept us from coming back at all. When we did return, to work on a script-writing contest for NPR, we learned that Frantz had been hospitalized after an apparent attempt at suicide, his optimism having yielded to a moment of despair.

Sample Exercise:

Write about an object in the room, without mentioning the name of that object, or create a scene that suggests an emotion, without actually naming that emotion. Afterwards, read your poem to the group, and see if they can guess what that object or emotion is.

Taking It to the Bridge

God, it's hot.
I've been on this road for hours.
Where am I going?
Why did I leave home?

Wait a second!
What's over there?
It's kids standing near a wall.
No, it's just a painting on the wall.

What does it say?
MIAMI BRIDGE CENTRAL.
If that painting hadn't been there,
I might still be on the streets today.

I give much thanks to the artist.
I've come in time to explore this place
I soon will call home.
I'm not sure about the people,

what to say to them, or where to begin.
I think, I think, this is my future.
Where does it end?

— Frantz, 18
Miami Bridge Central

School days

The last day I went to school
these were the sounds I heard:
Laughing, yelling, screaming, talking;
fighting, torment, pencils on paper;
snoring, hitting, tapping fingertips
on desks; desks skitting and scraping
on the rugged floor. Eating;
lockers slamming; rulers hitting
and slapping the chalkboards.
And at the end of the day,
buses driving away;
fingernails on chalkboards.

— Dee, 16
Capital City Youth Services, Tallahassee

Ain't It a Shame

Ain't it a shame
for kids to get beat up.
Moms and dads sometimes
really screw up.

Smoke crack like
it ain't no thang.
Then they beat up their kids.
Ain't it a shame.

Children cry,
they do not lie.
Moms and dads
don't even realize.

Kid goes to school
and tells the teacher.
Mom goes to church
and lies to the preacher.

—Antonio, 16
Great Oaks Village, Orlando

That Kid Ran Away

That kid ran away.
He was no good.
So much for him,
that old rotten dog.
Soon he will find out
the meaning of betrayal
and hatred. Soon this old dog
will know there are other
ways of getting food
than gnawing on an old bone.

"Stop that!
Get out of here!
Get a life!
Grow up, young dog,"
the old woman said.

> *— Sandra, 16*
> *PACE Center for Girls, Orlando*

Rules

There are so many rules
that can't be changed.

Be in your seat,
Silence when the bell rings!
Raise your hand.
Recognize the teacher.
Be polite.
Be considerate of others.

And always be neat.
Don't jiggle your earrings.
Oh man.
Oops, there goes my beeper.
Psych!
Oh brother.

Say No! to those school rules!

> *— Mevonda, 16*
> *PACE Center for Girls, Orlando*

Outside My Window

Blue-eyed baby dolls
and black little curls,
water spickets that run all day,
as we watch the rain flow,
flowing down on the minimum-wage houses
that can't afford new roof tops.
The grass is always greener
on the other side.
(What is the other side?
The other side of what?)
This big fish bowl of a world.
And the nasty motor vehicles.
And the crap from the pooper scooper
that no one picked up.

— Heather, 16
PACE Center for Girls, Jacksonville

Life in the Fast Lane

Chilling on the streets,
Selling heart beat,
Trying to make a dollar for my lil babe.

But one day, I must say,
I gotta get a job because this ain't the way.
Mom on my back.
Dad on crack.
Brothers on the street, trying Jack.

This type of shit happens all the time.
You got to get yours, and I got to get mine.

— Chris, 19
YouthBuild, Tallahassee

Tick Toc

The clock struck four.
The man dressed all snazzy
walked onto the street,
as this homeless creep
ran by and stole his watch.
The dog was sitting by a hydrant
scratching his ticks.
The little boy played with fire
and was shot into orbit.
The baby ate a napkin.
And the punk rocker wore mascara.
All on a September rainy day.

— *Sandra, 16*
PACE Center for Girls, Orlando

Meet Her at Arnette

I meet her at Arnette House.
She's pretty and sweet and nice.
Her eyes are blue like the sea.
Her hair makes me crazy.
Her eyes make me sparkle.
When I leave this place,
I'll always remember her.

—James, 12
Arnette House, Ocala

On Site

Being on site
I bam with my hammer
with all my might.

I drive a nail
like the judge
who sent me to jail.

But when it is wet,
I'd rather build a deck.

— Chris, 18
YouthBuild, Tallahassee

10

I Miss

I miss my home,
the sound of my mom calling us,
telling us to get up or
"Let's eat!"
Even telling us to quiet down.
The sound of my sister fussing at me,
my cousins asking to come in my room and play Sega,
their mom calling them,
"It's time to go," she would say,
and they would get upset because they wanted
to stay with me and play.

The sound of my dad telling me there's a phone call for me.

I miss my friends knocking on my window,
wanting me to come outside or come to their house.
I miss my birth mother because she died last year
before I went on summer vacation.
I miss my family because I didn't spend time with them,
except for the funeral, which was heartbreaking.

It shouldn't be heartbreaking because I was away
from them for six months.

But I still remember it like it was yesterday.
My mom reaching for me when they came and got me.
I was crying for her, but they took me away
too fast for her to grab me.
I miss my father.
He died before I was born.
I miss my family.

— Travis, 16
Capital City Youth Services, Tallahassee

Saying Goodbye

As I look at ya'll, I think to myself,
"how much I will miss you."
But, then again, I think how much
you were mean to me, and if you were here,
this is how I would describe you:

You are strong and manly,
but loving too.
You are so bright and smart,
but crazy too.
You have hair so wavy and brown but
so kinky too.

To me, you are worth more than chocolate
and all the money in the universe.

You are tall, dark, and good looking.
You have a smile that would
take the place of the Mona Lisa.
You are worth more than all the Lambourghinis
on the planet.

You are short and greedy,
but so cute too.
You are so obnoxious,
but loveable too.
You have eyes of diamonds and hair of gold.

You have one small dot
on the bottom of your right leg.
I call you Little Man,
and you call me DeeDee.

This is how I describe you.

— Dee, 16
Capital City Youth Services, Tallahassee

I Ain't Leaving

I ain't leaving.
I am going to be all alone.
I'm going to do
all the chores on my own.
I ain't leaving. What will I do,
when everyone's going
to be saying tootaloo?

> — *Serita, 14*
> *Youth & Family Connection, Clearwater*

I am Leaving

I am leaving, and my name is Paul.
I did not come to this shelter to have a ball.
I came here for help and things like that.
And now I'm leaving. What a drat!
I think this shelter has helped me much
with my attitude, behavior and such.
When I am out of here and back at home,
I'll be in the neighborhood with nowhere to roam.
While I was here, I didn't miss home a bit.
And now I'm going home. — Hell now, squash that shit!

> — *Paul, 14*
> *Youth & Family Connection, Clearwater*

II. Group Poems

Contexts:

Often, we encounter situations in the shelter in which participants are in transition and have had little time to get to know one another. The major challenge for Runaway with Words, *then, is to create an atmosphere of community and trust, so that the writers around the table feel comfortable enough to share their thoughts and creative work. As part of our introduction, we assign a group poem, in which everyone writes a stanza and then combines that stanza with others in the room to make a larger poem — somewhat in the tradition of the barn raising or quilting bee, where cooperation makes a larger project possible. We usually find, after we have completed this part of the workshop, that everyone is relaxing, beginning to be interested in each other's stories, and discovering that they have a lot in common.*

Anecdotes:

One of the group poems we use is the name rap, where everyone makes up a stanza giving their name and saying something simple or funny about themselves. This exercise has always worked as an ice breaker, but it occasionally has called attention to the musical limitations of the workshop leaders, who may fumble at directions or get caught in their efforts to fake an expertise they do not have. On one occasion, a desperate teacher asked if someone in the circle could help with the rhythm, and a young man named Roderick began thumping his fists on the desk, one-two, one-two-three, obviously familiar with the way things go. The stanzas that followed fit perfectly into the simple 2/3 time, and we realized that we had a skilled group of rappers on our hands, ones used to coming up with energetic rhymes. The miracle of this discovery was enhanced by our understanding that this group of students was not reputed to have many skills at all. In the context of their own culture, however, they were experts, and they easily shared with us what they knew.

Sample Exercise:

Write a poem stanza, using the following form:
    My name is [write out your name or nickname]
    That rhymes with [a rhyme that helps describe you]
    I come from/like to [where you come from/what you like to do]
    And I [something else you do or don't do]

My Name Is...

My name is Elmer.
That rhymes with Homer.
I like to irritate staff.
And then I laugh.

My name is Juliee.
That rhymes with bully.
I come from Tacoma.
And it has a nice aroma.

My name is Tee.
That rhymes with Nike.
I come from Arnette
And I like to eat.

My name is Chris.
That rhymes with kiss.
I like to swim.
And I do things on a whim.

My name is Bridgett.
That rhymes with be it.
I come from Chicago.
And I like to go for it.

My name is Fat Rat.
That rhymes with mad cat.
I like Big Macs
and from Big Macs I eat Kit Kats.

My name is Denham.
Yes, I'm passionate like venom.
I come from Basin Street,
And I like to eat meat.

My name is Amp.
That rhymes with ramp.
I come from Tallahassee,
And I think it's classy.

> — *Elmer, 14*
> *Juliee, 16*
> *Tee, 15*
> *Chris, 15*
> *Bridgett, 16*
> *Fat Rat, 13*
> *Denham, 18*
> *Amp, 18*
> *(various sites)*

I Remember a Time

I remember sitting in an open field.
It was the middle of July.
Everything was quiet.
I was happy to get away
from the chaos.

I remember playing on the beach
when the sun was hanging high in the sky.
How the mountains of ocean
crashed in and washed away
my castle of sand.

I remember catching
an 8 lb. bass.
When the day was nice,
flowers were blooming.
How the water was warm,
how the fish gave me a fight.

I remember going to the mall
with my friend who always ate
in one particular place.
When I was broke
and didn't have any money,
all I had to do was ask
and a penny, a nickel, and a dollar
would come my way.

I remember walking outside
when spring arrived,
when the birds chirped and
the smell of fresh roses filled the air.
How the wind blew through my hair
and whistled in my ear.
I looked at the sky, how peaceful
the world seemed.

I remember going hunting with my father
on Saturdays and Sundays.

I love the smell of discharged gunpowder
or the musky smell of ducks
already dead and gone.

— Jennifer, 15
Diana, 14
James, 15
Tee, 15
Bridgett, 16
Brian, 14
(various sites)

I Am The Child

I am the child who came out
of my mother's womb
so many years ago.

I am the child who knows best.

I am the child who talked
on the phone last night.

I am the child who went to see
JT and 2 Live Crew last night.

I am the child who didn't feel
like coming to school today,
but I came anyway.

I am the child who learns
the rules of life.

I am the child who feels
and makes others feel.

I am the child who rebels,
and makes her life fit her.

I am the child who is looking
at you. In the light, in the dark,
I still see you.

> — *Tasha, Kellie, Sylvia, Keyshonda,*
> *Kim, Kimber, Sheree*
> *PACE Center for Girls, Tallahassee*

I Remember

I remember when I was in the second grade
and we had just moved to Gainesville
from New York. I was about seven or eight,
and we lived at Palm Bay apartments,
and I went to Williams Elementary.
I would ride the bus home,
and my mom would meet me at the bus stop.
I would go in and change and go out
to the pool and rescue the bees and bugs
that were drowning. I felt like I
was doing something really good and
to be proud of. It was good. I would
just sit by the pool and do that
until it got dark.

— Andrew
Interface Youth Program, Gainesville

I Remember Daddy

I remember Daddy and what he meant to me.
I remember Daddy and what he said to me.
I can see him
in his white robe walking on the Golden
shore to join the million voices
in the angels' great choir.
Jesus must be happy to have my Daddy there
to join the angels' great band.

I remember the night the news came to me,
I cried and prayed and asked how on earth
could it be?
Daddy was so wonderful,
but awful too.
He was loved by all and hated too.
I remember Daddy and what he done to me.

— Dee, 16
Capital City Youth Services, Tallahassee

There Never Was a Time When This Was Not So

Today my name is Chameleon.
I know she is flexible, changeable, brilliant.
There never was a time when this was not so.

Today my name is eagle who flies.
I know I have a free spirit.
There never was a time when this was not so.

Today my name is eagle.
I know that I am quick and cunning.
There never was a time when this was not so.

Today my name is cat.
I know that cats like to sleep a lot.
There never was a time when this was not so.

Today my name is Alf.
I know Alf eats a lot.
There never was a time when this was not so.

— Daphne (Staff)
Sarah (Staff)
Paul, 14
Jeanette, 14
Tommy, 17
Youth and Family Connection,
Clearwater and St. Petersburg

In The Mirror

I see a nice young man,
doing the best he can.
He's sitting back,
making up a plan
of what he wants
to be in life —
to have a nice job,
three kids and a wife.
If I'm going somewhere in life,
I've got to go far.
so I'm saving up my money,
to buy a nice car.
I'm always thinking
about my friends down under.
They are dead,
that's why I wonder.

I see a black, beautiful, young lady
with beautiful eyes and a cut
in the corner of my left eye.
I see a funny shaped nose.
I wonder, will I always look like this?

I see this red-eyed black guy
with dreads in his hair,
ears pierced, and
a Malcolm X shirt on,
with hair on his chin,
chewing on some gum.
Everyone says
I look like my dad.
But I'm looking in the mirror
trying to see,
who can see me? I wonder.
I see
what could be a mystery,
what might have been changed
through the years of misery.

Even though I don't regret anything,
would I ever want to go back
and change something?

I wonder. . .

I see a psycho when I get mad.
I see a good-looking young man
when I am straight-faced.

I wonder if I am going
to meet the right person.

I see loveliness
here in this mirror.
Sexy eyes, a pretty smile,
and a cute nose.
I notice, though, I need
my hair done and
I need a little make-up.
I wonder, sometimes,
what's really going on
under all this stuff?

I see long black and brown nappy hair,
big brown eyes, and a manly stare.
I see a blue shirt with short sleeves,
a big wide nose from which to breathe.
I see the family resemblance to a brother named Wayne,
with the smooth brown skin, just smooth and plain.

> — *Nate, 16*
> *Latoya, 17*
> *Roderick, 18*
> *Ginger, 18*
> *Kurtis, 17*
> *Lakesha, 17*
> *Marcell, 18*
> *YouthBuild, Tallahassee*

III. Self-portraits

Contexts:

One of the first and most sweeping generalizations we have heard about shelter kids is that they suffer from low self-esteem. While this diagnosis may be accurate, we discover in getting to know them that part of their silence comes from a respect for their own feelings, that they care enough about themselves to avoid the emotional bruising they have come to expect from adults. So, sometimes, they sit silently, with their backs turned to the circle, sometimes they create elaborate masks behind which their more vulnerable selves can hide. The personality we think we are getting to know turns out to be quite different from the personality we discover in the end. A young boy who on one day has convinced us he's a monster can on another day be completely docile and kind.

Anecdotes:

Alfred seemingly had a problem with women. His counselors informed us that, given his emotional problems and history, he was at risk of doing some harm. Meeting him, we discovered a bright young man, growing into puberty, alarmed at his own ungainliness. He was willing to write about this awkwardness, metaphorically casting himself as a pig or a whale and imagining their sense of the world and themselves. We encouraged him to write, without confirming or calling attention to his need for self-deprecation. As the workshop continued, Alfred gained confidence in his writing and spent less time feeling bad about who he was, where he came from, what he needed or missed. Although he sat somewhat outside of the circle, he treated us with warmth and respect, writing many fine poems in response to the exercises given. Several years later, when he showed up at the shelter across town, my student teachers were the ones to meet and work with him. They spoke enthusiastically about the proud young man who wrote with conviction about his determination and was a knowledgeable voice in workshop proceedings.

Sample Exercise:

Look into a mirror and write a poem describing what you see there. Picture a landscape, an everyday object, or an animal you know and describe it in such a way that it represents a familiar emotion, perhaps one you are feeling now.

My Determination

I am a hard worker.
I do not pick cotton.
I do not say scrawberries or screet.

My nose is not pointy.
My eyes are not blue.
My hair is not a stringy golden wheat.

My nose is wide.
My eyes are brown.
My hair is wool.
I am not a tantalizing tan or a sun-kissed
bronze.

I am a child of God.
My name is **Alfred**, and
My Determination is to be Free.

— Alfred, 16
Capital City Youth Services, Tallahassee

I Like to Paint

I always wanted to paint,
but my dad always told me I can't.

Then one day I painted my room,
and it was full of bloom.

It was the color red that
matches the rail of my bed.

The floor was made of wood.
I had done something I knew I could.

— Derrick, 18
YouthBuild, Tallahassee

Anger in the Heart

They say anger is bad for your heart.
Then why do I let myself get so hot?
Do I just hold it in until I split,
or do I let it out and slowly die?

— Melissa, 13
BEACH House, Daytona Beach

Her Life

Her life was like this,
      white and brown,
      smooth and round.
She is short and little, with a light weight.
She has a crystal point that looks like snow.
      It feels very hard,
      and it has rough edges.

          — Keyshonda, 17
             PACE Center for Girls, Tallahassee

Her Life

Her life was like a jagged rock,
hard and cold,
with few if any smooth spots.
Dark and threatening,
with many places
where one could get hurt.
This is what her life was like.

          — Kimber, 15
             PACE Center for Girls, Tallahassee

The Color of Secrets

Come here!
Slap, pound, bang!
Go to your room!
These are the sounds I heard while I was young.
One day, I'm white.
The next, I'm purple and blue.
I go to school with shame and secrets,
hoping to hide my purple and blue marks.
But I stretch one good time,
and the teacher asks questions.
The next day, I have the "Home Recking Service" on my tail.
Three weeks later, I have a so-so report card,
and then I hear, "Pop, Pop, Pound" again,
and I have more purple and blue marks on me again.
I never reveal my secret.
But then I have a white scar to go with
my beautiful purple and blue marks.

— Dee, 16
Capital City Youth Services, Tallahassee

Questionable Judgement

I have questionable judgement
about things in the world.
A questionable judgement about
ice cream with swirls.
I have questionable judgement
of how life works.
A questionable judgement of how
guys can be jerks.

— Kaila, 16
PACE Center for Girls, Orlando

Rebellion

I don't wanna write
I wanna sit in a corner
I wanna sing
but I don't wanna harmonize
I done forgot all about words
though I just read a dictionary
I wanna whirl
yet stay in one place

— Chris, 16
Capital City Youth Services, Tallahassee

Too

There are too many things
"too" describes about me.
As in, "too big" and (that's not a gig),
and I do eat like a pig.
— Too silly? — Guess who?
— What should I do?
There are just too many things
"too" describes about me,
always starting with a great big "B."

— Alfred, 13
Capital City Youth Services, Tallahassee

Broken Fingernail

Sometimes I feel like
a broken fingernail
which has broken high
to the nailbed.
A fingernail that didn't
break completely off,
just hangs there,
bends, pains.
A fingernail that somebody
tries to pull off,
but never breaks from me.
A fingernail already broken,
but never lets go.
A fingernail that people cry over
as their own loss.
A fingernail that is guilty for breaking,
but I am the one who broke it.
A fingernail that is broken, and silent.
Sometimes I feel like a fingernail,
already broken,
but never lets go.

— Rachel, 16
PACE Center for Girls, Orlando

Who I Am

I am a Heart without sorrow,
A Bird without fear.
I fly around and around,
Not hearing a sound.

Oh, how I wish
Life wasn't so hard,
you see. . . many different things
— I know not —
But have much to learn.

So, I will continue to fly
As long as God lets me,
And with Him in me and I in Him,
So will I find my Destination.

> — *Lamont, 20*
> *YouthBuild, Tallahassee*

If This Rock

If this rock came to life,
it would be
the crystal blue river
crashing up against the river walls.

> — *Jennifer, 17*
> *PACE Center for Girls, Tallahassee*

Vampire

The blood dripped from his lips
after sucking her love for him out.
The two teeth marks, with not
a drop of blood left on the skin.
The woman fell to her knees
and wept to have his power.
He hit her to the floor again.
He raked his monstrous teeth
across her neck, this time
sucking the life out of her.
Then with a flash of lightning,
the cape went over his handsome
face, and he was gone.
The woman, dead; the victim of the vampire.
The only thing the woman wanted
was love, and it didn't matter
from whom. Just someone to care.
Well, she got what she wanted,
someone to care, but he cared
so much, he took her life for his.

Can this happen?
If so, let it be done to me.

> — *Star, 17*
> *PACE Center for Girls, Orlando*

IV. Letters and Conversations

Contexts:

Many of these young people leave unresolved emotional situations behind them when they run. Many want to see or be able to talk with the person they have hurt by running. Many want to figure out why their parents are violent or troubled or unable to give them the love they need. They want to explain or express their own motives and feelings, even though the situation makes it impossible for them to do so face-to-face. For them, the idea that a poem can be a conversation with an absent person is a revelation and a way of dealing with their isolation and frustration. They realize in the process how clear they are on what they want to say and how clear they are on what that other person would say in return. If there is no one for the child to worry about, to love, and wish to be reunited with, as is sometimes the case, there is at least a dream that there could be, and making up an audience, someone to love, to write to or talk with, provides comfort in a world where such associations are commonly discounted or deemed impossible.

Anecdotes:

Evelin wanted to write a letter to her mother, but she was frustrated and angry because she couldn't write. Her emotions quickly turned to tears at the seeming impossibility of putting words in order on the page. Janet took her aside, asking her who she wanted to write to and what she wanted to say. As Evelin dictated, Janet wrote down Evelin's words. With serious learning disabilities, Evelin was not expected to have much promise as a writer, but she clearly knew what she wanted to say and to whom, and it mattered very much to her to be able to express her feelings on paper or out loud. Her desire made for a touching poem to her mother, and a strong example for the other participants, for whom the task was not so difficult.

Sample Exercise:

Read William Carlos Williams' "This is Just to Say" and talk about it as a note the poet may have written to his wife and stuck on the refrigerator, apologizing for having eaten all the plums. Write a poem in the form of a letter or note to someone you care for, telling them what you want to tell them. Then, write another poem in the voice of that other person, saying what you think they would say in response.

Dear Mom / Dear Evelin

Dear Mom:

How are you?
What are you doing?
Today has been depressing.
I would like to be home,
to be happy
with my mom and dad.

Dear Evelin:

I am doing fine.
Today I read your poem.
I would like for you
to come home,
but I don't think the judge
would let you.

— Evelin, 18
Arnette House, Ocala

This is Just to Say

This is just to say
I'm sorry for the trouble,
heartache and pain
I put you through. I know
you tried to raise us,
and yet we do you so wrong.
I know I don't express how much
I care for you, but I really do
love you a lot.
I'm sorry you had to sit up
in the midnight hour
and cry and wonder what
I was doing. But now,
I see why you always fuss
and get mad at me.
And I thank you for that.
And I thank you for taking care
of me all these years.
I love you.

— Tanesha, 16
Haven Poe Runaway Center, Tampa

A Mother's Answer

I read your letter,
and it really touched me.
It's hard for a mother
to accept the fact
that her only daughter
is growing up.
I'm not the only one
who helped you, taught you.
You taught me a lot,
and I thank you.
You mean the world to me,
and I love you.

— Jennifer, 15
Haven Poe Runaway Center, Tampa

Hey Girl

Hey girl,
clean my shoes,
and tell your mom,
I say hi and bye.

But I will be back
to get my money.
See you.

Give me my money
before I blow up your name.

— Elmer, 14
Youth Crisis Center South, Jacksonville

Mommy I'm in Your Tummy

Mommy I'm in your tummy,
and the month is only May.
I'm only the size of a grain.

Now it's February, and I
would have been a day old now.

You didn't give me a chance at life,
Mommy. I know you would have
loved me, Mommy. I love you.

> — *K.K.R, 15*
> *Haven Poe Runaway Center, Tampa*

This is Just to Say

How sorry I am
that the words
we have shared
have made an empty
space between us.

This is just to say,
I really do care,
and raising my hand
was not my intent.

Forgive me someday soon,
for I long to fill the empty space
with love that I hold deep in my heart.

> — *Diana, 14*
> *Haven Poe Runaway Center, Tampa*

Last Night

About last night,
what I did was not right.
I can only hope you forgive me.
Right now, I need you, I hope you need me.
Where do I go from here? Did I become a stranger?
Have I put your life in any type of danger?
Due to circumstances, I must flee the scene.
If you see me again, don't ask where I've been.
Oh, about last night, I'm sorry.

— Frantz, 18
Miami Bridge Central

Lessons

The hardest lesson in life to learn
is which bridge to turn,
and which bridge to burn.

The best thing about being young
is that you are not experienced enough
to know that you cannot   possibly do
the things you are doing.

— Kimber, 15
PACE Center for Girls, Tallahassee

What I've Got to Say

I ran away from this treacherous place,
which you probably already know.

I'm just saying goodbye.

I have to leave; no time to say why.

—*Julia, 12*
Capital City Youth Services, Tallahassee

A Message from Fat Rat

I'm sorry, Honey,
I have to work a double shift.
I guess we will have to go
to the movie tomorrow.

—*Fat Rat, 13*
Miami Bridge, Homestead

A Message to Sandra
(Who Wants to Be a Teacher)

I think I am
nice and neat. Do you
think I am
nice? I love
myself as I am.

I am twelve.
Do you, Sandra, think
I am thirty?

> — *Byron, 12*
> *Capital City Youth Services, Tallahassee*

Questions

You are asking me questions,
and I hear you.
When you talk down to me,
I hear you,
but when you talk to me,
I listen to you.

> — *Autumn,*
> *PACE Center for Girls, Jacksonville*

Bouncing Babies

When an infant grows, it starts to bounce,
and when they bounce, different things come out.
Sometimes, even words you don't understand.
They say something like Blaa Bla Loo Cooo.
And if you can understand that, please tell me.

Babies are people. They may not be as big
or think as us, but we're lucky for that
because if they did, their words wouldn't be
Blaa Bla Loo Cooo. They would say something
like, "Stay away, you ugly thing," or worse.

Today, everything bounces.
But don't let it be words or hatred.

— Dee, 16
Capital City Youth Services, Tallahassee

V. Pictures and Words

Contexts:

Our memories come to us in pictures — scenes that carry with them significances more intense than simple description can manage. Words and phrases, carefully chosen, reproduce the power of those scenes, conveying to others associations that otherwise would remain unexpressed. The workshop is a place where the unbelieveable happens on a regular basis, in the sense that we discover more about ourselves than we thought it possible to know and that we speak beyond our assumed level of skill. The expressions of these young people are rich with desire, and the aim of the workshop is to demonstrate the positive value of their experiences and dreams.

Anecdotes:

When we first met Eleina at PACE Orlando, she was wearing a SONY walkman. Eyes fixed on the wall, earphones clamped to her ears, she expressed total indifference to what we had to say. When the earphones came off, she still wanted us to understand that we were stupid, that this poetry thing wasn't helpful, and that she really preferred her own music to ours. I'm not sure what changed Eleina's mind — or even if her mind was changed — but the person we got to know was totally different from the person we encountered at this first meeting. When it came time to decide who would participate in the Runaway with Words *performance at Walt Disney World, Eleina chose to stay and work with us. She translated parts of June Jordan's "Menu" poem into Spanish, giving it a multicultural dimension, and she wrote a number of fine poems herself. She became a leader in choreography, insisting on certain specific movements and providing cues for recitation. In a room full of adults and peers, she read her own work with pride, kept the long line of PACE girls together, and impressed everyone with her confidence and style.*

Sample Exercise:

Prepare a stack of 3x5 index cards with cut out pictures and lines from recent magazines and newspapers. Shuffle the cards and have each participant choose one. Write a poem from the chosen card, whatever the words suggest. If nothing happens, choose another card. In the end, each participant should tell the group what card they chose and read their poem response.

Who is That Man

Who is that man?
I can't tell you,
because I don't know.
He's just a man,
walking down the street
with a bag, who's going somewhere
to see someone, but I can't
tell you, because I don't
know.

— Eleina, 16
PACE Center for Girls, Orlando

Can You Smell It

Can you smell it
over there in this fresh
cut grass. Berries
smell good, don't they?
I bet they taste good.
Go ahead, try one, they're
all nice and good they
grew right out here
in the sunny fresh grass.
Just look, there are
millions of them:
shiny red, purple, blue,
and black.
They're very juicy.
I bet you can taste
the juice in your mouth,
all sweet and tasty.

— La Tasha, 13
Capital City Youth Services, Tallahassee

Flows Like Water

It's soft and mellow,
flows like water.
The sun beats down
and it shines like glitter.
The grass stands green
from nourishment.
The wind runs through the trees
and sings its own song.
The birds are relaxed,
as they just fly along.

— *Pam, 17*
PACE Center for Girls, Tallahassee

When Frogs Dance

She says she'll go out with you
when frogs dance, meaning never
in our life will you have a chance.
So, what does that thought bring
to your mind? You won't have her
in the future or even back in time.
So even if frogs danced, you
wouldn't have a chance, because
it's not in her mind, and she
wouldn't find the time.

— *Kaila, 16*
PACE Center for Girls, Orlando

Lumpfish

Soaring through the ocean depths
with strength, agility, grace.
Sometimes even; sometimes noticeable,
the stride can change any moment.

There is no particular reason
for the beauty of the lumpfish.

— *Daphne (Staff)*
Youth & Family Connection South,
St. Petersburg

Impact

A water balloon will bust
when it's hitting the floor.
An orange, as it falls to the floor.
A bottle, when it's thrown hard
and hits the road.
A rock, as a hammer hits it.

— *Travis, 15*
Capital City Youth Services, Tallahassee

Mother and Son

Here, you see a mother and a son.
They look like they're bored and ain't having no fun.
Here, you see a son and his mother.
They look like they're dead, oh brother.
And the little boy is ready for bed.
That's what I see when I look at this card.
Now, let me be off to play in the yard.

> — *Paul, 14*
> *Youth & Family Connection North,*
> *Clearwater*

Psycho Suicide

Farewell to a talented psycho, I said,
as those morbid thoughts pulsed through my head.
He was more than merely Norman Bates —
my victims now, past the cemetery gates.
The hate, the anger, no remorse at all.
Down in Hell, it's a never-ending fall.
They stepped in my world and took a ride.
They'll always remember the terror inside.
Rest in Peace is a thing of the past.
The pain, so long; the death, so fast.
Ripping flesh and screams of no hope.
my body is now dangling from a rope.

> — *Lisa, 16*
> *The Village School, Orlando*

Cool Cloudy Day

It was a cool, cloudy day,
wind blowing at a slow pace,
sun just rising upon the gray skies.
The instructor works. We're building.
You can hear a loud sound
like drills driving, saws cutting wood,
as people hang sheetrock.

— Shekalla, 18
YouthBuild, Tallahassee

Building a House

The first day I came, I had to wear a tool pouch.
I heard loud sounds. I saw hammers going back and forth.
Men were hustling, painting.
The sun was shining, everyone was sweating.
We went on through the whole three months doing that,
and the house was finished.
I couldn't believe I had helped build a house.

— Latoya, 17
YouthBuild, Tallahassee

Words and Thoughts: 1945-1993

It's a dream come true.
My thoughts, my words
in magazines, in books.

Hurrah! Hurrah!
There's nothing more I want to do now.

I'll be famous!!
I'll be rich!!
I'll stock up on paper, pencils,
                and pens.
And write more and more
                and MORE!

Everyone will know me.
Everyone will know my words...
Everyone will know my thoughts...

Is that really all I wanted?
Hmmmmm?

> — *Dale (Staff)*
> *The Village School, Orlando*

Fashionable Shopping

One weekend my friends and I
took a trip to the mall
to get some fashionable clothes
and some fashionable earrings
for a party they had invited us to,
and my outfit was tan, with
eggshell colored earrings.

> — *Eleina, 16*
> *PACE Center for Girls, Orlando*

VI. Body Talk

Contexts:

*Teenagers are highly aware of their bodies, often fright-
ened by the transformations they are experiencing on the
way to adulthood. The emotional conflicts and confusions
brought on by physical change make meditations on the body
emotionally difficult, but creatively rewarding. To a great
degree, the distinction between love and physical intimacy is
not at all clear to these young people, and in cases where
abuse is a part of their personal history, the confusion can be
very deep indeed. Nevertheless, it is necessary for them to
confront the image of their physical selves and attempt to find
self-definition and control. This process may be long and slow
— longer and slower than the workshop can accommodate
— but poetry gives them a way to begin and a method of
looking at the issues. The strength of metaphor in such
therapeutic situations is that it offers a route of indirection,
whereby a person can express figuratively what would other-
wise be impossible to say.*

Anecdotes:

It was a Saturday morning gathering, and we didn't know each other very well. The kids were new to the shelter and somewhat subdued by the experience of displacement, while the counselors were uncertain about poetry in general and how their charges would respond to us. As we huddled together doing our writing, we gradually began to feel safe with each other and to enjoy the results of our experiments. One of the participants, a willowy 15-year-old named Beverly, brightened with the opportunity to display her talents. Quiet but quick in her responses, she wrote a poem called "My Feet," which we later included in our Runaway with Words *workbook. Six months later, we ran into her again at the Florida Network's FACT conference, where she read "My Feet" and performed her rendition of Maya Angelou's "Life Doesn't Frighten Me at All." By then aware of some of the reasons why Beverly should have been afraid, we marvelled at her courage and self-posession, the simplicity with which she rendered these traits in words.*

Sample Exercise:

Choose a body part, such as eyes, nose, hands, or feet, and write a poem about it so that it helps us understand the whole person better. You may write about yourself or someone else, but it is preferable to start with a self-portrait.

My Feet

I have these brown and yellow things
on the end of my legs.
I sometimes wonder
what these things are.
They're real funny looking.

But they take me to the places
that I wish to go.
And they let me play the games
that my friends sometimes play using their legs.

On the top of these brown and yellow things,
is skin that is sometimes dry and rough.
On the end of these funny things,
are dead cells called nails which grow long and hard.
But these funny looking brown and yellow things called feet
keep me on my toes and standing tall.

— Beverly, 14
Family Service Program, Orlando

Shoes

Are shoes just pads on your feet
so that you won't hurt your babyish skin?
Or are they like carpets so you won't touch
the hard floor?

You should be comfortable wearing your shoes,
so be proud of them.
Don't hurt them or wear them out.
Even if shoes are not alive,
they're yours,
so treat them like butterflies.

—*Joseph, 14*
Family Services Program, Orlando

I Like My Hands

I like my hands,
'cause I can grip the mike and entertain like a band,
use the movement as I rap,
get the people jumping as they begin to clap.
My hands are the greatest hands of all.
They help me lift things up and knock down walls.
My hands are the smoothest things,
And no other rapper could dare to hang.
Hands are used in every way,
they help me every day.
Hands won't fail you, never-ever,
grabbing the mic with my hands makes me feel better.
They help you rub down the opposite sex.
Sometimes they help you play.
You can wave hello and hi,
But at this point I'll just say bye.

—*Ronald, 16*
Family Services Program, Orlando

My Nose

When I wake up, my nose
smells fresh air.

When a beautiful, sexy woman
wears perfume,

I can smell it forever
and ever.

—Jimmy, 13
Family Services Program, Orlando

My Eyes

These eyes, so bright and wise,
I can't help but think, when
I look in the blue sky,
the creativity and sensitivity
that you can see,
tells you all about me.

The wonderful, warm colors
they bring, find me
joy in everything.
My eyes, so shy, so timid,
so pure, I'm so glad they're mine
I'll always adore.

— Lakena, 15
PACE Center for Girls, Orlando

The Hands

My hands remind me
of my mother's working hands,
always busy caring for her children.
These hands, always holding, working, hitting,
touching, and caressing. The fingers are short,
but beautiful. I could never do without them.

— Julette (Staff)
Family Services Program, Orlando

Hands

Powerful, but gentle, best describes the part
of my body that ends with fingers.
Coarsely, but warmly, they reach out to strangers.
Long, but short, compared to a mile,
but, if ever hugged with them, you're sure to smile.
My hands are dark, my palms are fair.
With them both, I enhance my career.
The beauty of the land
was partly planted by my hands.

— Karl (Staff)
Family Services Program, Orlando

VII. Animals and Totems

Contexts:

We find among them an unusual number of beautiful names — Hope, Kaila, Diamond, Moses, Tyrone — suggesting their uniqueness and the sense of promise they must have inspired when they were born. This promise may or may not have been borne out as they grew. More often than not, it evaporated in the face of family friction, disappointment, and suffering. Many of them have taken on new names as a result — Black X, Pookie, Fat Rat, Star — and, with those names, a sense of their own individuality and power. We want the poem to help them look at who they are and to reestablish a kinship between themselves and others. The Native American tradition where individuals earn their names through identification with an animal seemed a potent example for this process.

Anecdotes:

Brian, we were told, had been arrested for having killed an alligator. We assumed he must be a violent and overbearing youth, a potential source of disruption in the workshop. When we met him, however, we discovered a small, though energetic, fourteen-year-old, obviously a product of an authoritative household and used to getting a rise out of people with his callous attitude toward death. For all his toughness, Brian had a sense of humor, and his no-nonsense writing and speaking style translated into some very good poems. We grew to like him. We hoped that he liked us. He seemed to be grateful, at least, for our ability to laugh at his jokes.

Sample Exercise:

Play a cassette of animal sounds, specifically of whales, loons, or wolves.
Write a poem translating into human language what you think the whales, loons or wolves are saying. Write a poem about an animal you like, which helps us understand more clearly your appreciation for that animal, what it says and does.

The Elephant

Once, there was a big elephant
who lived in a wild jungle, and
everywhere he went, he would always
flatten grapes and eat grass.
He was the noisiest thing in that jungle,
but he loved eating peanuts
and drinking water and playing in mud puddles —
and he hated taking baths.

— Paula, 16
PACE Center for Girls, Orlando

What I Think the Whales are Saying

There was this mother whale and baby whale.
The mother whale got caught in a fisherman's net
that had been set. The mother whale called out
to her young in sadness, and the baby whale yelled back
in madness. After the mother had been taken away,
the baby was left out to stray. Having no one to love
and care for was his worst nightmare.

— Alfred, 13
Capital City Youth Services, Tallahassee

Eohippus

Eohippus ran really fast
on his big feet.
He ran from dinosaurs.
Eohippus had the skull
of a modern horse.
He was carnivorous.

— Brian, 14
Capital City Youth Services, Tallahassee

A Horse Comes in Any Color

A Horse comes in any color,
but, oh, brother, this horse is blue.
Lord, what should I do?
What can the horse do besides stay blue?
Can it jump without landing with a thump?
Can I take it to a show?
What can I name it, Moe?
Can it trot proudly without disturbing the crowd,
because I think the color blue is loud?

—Alfred, 13
Capital City Youth Services, Tallahassee

Animals

I don't like animals,
because some bite and
eat you up,
and some are just ugly,
but some are cute.

> — *Shadrina, 12*
> *Capital City Youth Services, Tallahassee*

Lions

Lions are fast
in the fields.
Lions are all around,
open to the seabreeze.
None are slow, all are fast.
They might just cross your path.

> — *Jessica, 11*
> *Capital City Youth Services, Tallahassee*

The Polkadotted Bug

The Polkadotted Bug shouted,
"Hey! I'm your father, so shut up!"

— Brian, 14
Capital City Youth Services, Tallahassee

Secrets

Helllloooo...
Hello, hello, hello.
I know a secret.
I know a secret.
Tell us!
Tell us!
The grey cocoons, the brown tadpoles,
              the hard-shelled eggs.
All hold beautiful secrets.
The oysters, the beehives, the womb,
All hold beautiful secrets.
When can we see them?
When can we know the secrets?
Only when it is time.

— Daphne (Staff)
Youth & Family Connection South,
St. Petersburg

VIII. Heroes

Contexts:

Hostility and cynicism are a defense against disappointment; passivity, a way of getting back at whatever hurts you. The workshop tries to discover meaningful experience, gather up memories and ideas that will sustain us in difficult times. Thus, we seek out role models, some example of someone who does not disappoint or betray. These role models may be personal or private, they may come from the culture at large, or they may be purely imaginary. For many, the ability to make good choices, to succeed in life, requires a creative sense of what is possible, a sufficient opening of the mind to let some hope take root. That we could look for or find answers to our own problems in someone else's experience comes as a novel surprise to many and starts the movement away from self-absorption and self-pity that civilizes and socializes us.

Anecdotes:

When eighteen-year-old Tommy failed to recognize the picture of Anita Hill he had drawn from our pile of flash cards, I wondered what kind of circumstances had isolated him from the newspaper, television, and radio reports that had flooded our daily lives. I had heard that he had been involved in some kind of cult before arriving at the shelter, which translated into a general defiance of all things "good." He didn't express hope for the future or have much energy for the workshop because he couldn't see that there was hope or purpose in either one. I wondered if Tommy's lack of social connectedness, his determined passivity, had anything to do with an absence of stories in his life, if some familiarity with the basic tales of our culture could have given him a point of reference from which to make choices and act. He never mentioned anyone or anything he believed in, but, after the workshop, he stood outside holding onto a girl he would miss when they sent him back home. Clearly, she was different from the rest, although he never explained how or why.

Sample Exercise:

Play a recording of a song about a hero (e.g., June Jordan's poem about "Sojourner Truth," sung by Bernice Reagon). Explain the hero's story and the values it represents. Then — think of someone you consider to be a hero, either someone you know or someone known by many, and write a poem about them. Choose a scene from their life which helps illustrate what you see in this individual.

Michael Jordan

Michael Jordan, my hero,
dunking the ball off the wall
into the basket from very far.
What a star —
my hero, Michael Jordan.

> — *Serita, 14*
> *Youth & Family Connection North,*
> *Clearwater*

My Hero is the X Man

My Hero is the X Man.
He goes through the night
helping kids. One night,
he was going to get me,
but a hero in a black jacket
helped me. He saved my life,
and he has a name, but he says
I cannot tell anyone.

> — *Elmer, 14*
> *Youth Crisis Center North, Jacksonville*

Harriet Tubman

Harriet was a fighting slave.
She was known for the freedom she gave.
She gave slaves freedom, rights,
and she always stayed out of sight.
She was also very smart,
but to me she was a piece of art.
Many people thanked her well
for getting them out of hell.

— Alfred, 13
Capital City Youth Services, Tallahassee

My Hero

I believe my hero
should be
everyone's hero.

Because this man
allowed things to
be equal.
He united white with black,
black with white.

This man had
every derogatory
thing said to him.

But he didn't let
this bring him down.
Oh no.
He said, he said, he said,
I got a dream.

This hero I believe in
is Martin Luther King.

— Tiffany, 16
PACE Center for Girls, Orlando

I Had a Dream

When I rode through the city
the other day,
I saw it was time
for a change.
Everyone should
be together.
We should unite
as one.
Color has nothing
to do with anything.
Everyone is
brainwashed.
Blacks over here...
whites over there.
I had a dream...
that someday
everyone would be together.
We all deserve
equal rights.
I had a dream...
That we could all
eat together.
Is color everything?
Everyone is a person inside.
If we were all blind...
would it matter?
But I'm sure
a white man would find something
to keep us away. I had a dream...

— Angela, 16
PACE Center for Girls, Orlando

Walter Cronkite

I like Walter Cronkite
because he's rich and famous
like all rich people are.
But the thing which sets him
above all rich people
is that he is smart and he's talented.
He's a very good actor
and above all,
the very nicest man in all the world.

— Brian, 14
Capital City Youth Services, Tallahassee

Rick Springfield

They laughed at you when you were young.
Your peers just didn't seem to care.
They did not give you half a chance
and would not treat you fair.

But later in your life,
fame and fortune came to be,
and now everyone was watching you on tv.
As I listened to your music on the radio,
you helped me to be happy with me.

— Sarah (Staff)
Youth & Family Connection South,
St. Petersburg

My Hero

Let me tell you of a hero to me.
My hero never was an astronaut or a scientist.
To be a doctor or lawyer, he didn't fit the mold.
He couldn't sing nor could he act.
No Pulitzer prizes; no, nothing like that.
My hero wiped my nose when it was runny
from being outside in the cold.
When I was hungry, he made sure
I had plenty to eat. When I got sleepy,
he made way for me to sleep.
He rewarded me when I did good
and chastised me when I was bad.
I didn't understand it then,
but I appreciate it now.
He always knew what was best for me somehow.
He supplied all of my needs and a few of my wants.
He taught me to be the very best I could be.
He's my hero and for that I'm glad.
He's known by another name,
but I call him Granddad.

— *Angelo (Staff)*
Youth Crisis Center North, Jacksonville

Malcolm X

Angry and intelligent.
Master of the English
            language,
with liberal doses of
            humor and arrogance.

Malcolm X, formerly Detroit Red,
            once just Malcolm Little,
stood before the crowd;
            the milling crowd, consisting
mainly of Negro women
            on their way to work,
and Negro children debating whether
            to go to school or attend
the once in a lifetime hooky party,
            which happens everyday.

Malcolm X, formerly Detroit Red,
            once just Malcolm Little,
stood before the crowd,
            expounding ideas of self-pride
and self-care,
and the notion that the status-quo
ain't cutting it no more.

Malcolm X, formerly Detroit Red,
          once just Malcolm Little,
stood before the crowd,
          a self-made man with conviction
and determination
          and desire, passionate burning
desire.
Angry and intelligent,
          master of the English Language,
with liberal doses of
          humor and arrogance,
some say too much arrogance.

> — *Cassandra (Staff)*
> *Youth & Family Connection South,*
> *St. Petersburg*

IX. The Numbers Game

Contexts:

*We process them in terms of categories and numbers —
"16 year old BF," "13 year old WM" — believing that such
labels give an accurate record of who they are, of what they
desire to be. Yet, what we look for in the workshop are non-
statistical moments, those points of contact when an indi-
vidual rediscovers the will to communicate. In Florida, there
are an average of 60,000 reported runaways each year;
nationally, that number swells to anywhere from 500,000 to
2,000,000. Each one of those numbers represents a child in
trouble, a child whose lack of direction and support puts him
or her at-risk of physical harm. Writing brings us to the table,
helps us focus on the issues that drive their lives and ours,
keeps us conscious of the human being behind this curious
urge to count.*

Anecdotes:

At seventeen, Hope had already experienced tragedy in the form of a friend's suicide and was still struggling with her sense of loss. She had written a poem about it, which her teachers and friends admired greatly, and, when we came to the workshop that day, they urged us to read it and tell them what we thought. We discovered in it an articulate young woman, troubled by the wastefulness of her friend's death, trying to discover what it meant to give up on her future and turn her back on those who had cared for her. She had a long way to go before she could fully accept what had happened, but Hope had decided that poetry helped. In the number assignment I gave them, she found another way of discussing her friend's death. I had been curious to find out the group's attitude toward numbers and the use of numbers to typify them. Her poem reminded me that any one day of the year, any number or statistic, could represent failure or fulfillment, depending on who was seeing it, whose experiences were taken into account.

Sample Exercise:

Think of a number that might have some significance in your life or day-to-day experience. Write a poem, in any form, rhymed or unrhymed, that has that number in it.

Seven

To think of seven is to dream of a lake,
where I see swans swimming around
in the form of a seven.

Heaven reminded me of love and truth;
I came from heaven on a golden number seven.

Life, love, joy, and peace can be taken away
in seven shots. We can give life in seven steps:

— Love
— Truth
— Honesty
— Trust
— Respect
— Caring

— A good life.

— Trecie, 15
PACE Center for Girls, Jacksonville

Nine

There's this art pad I know,
the only way he can work
is to make a sign
to find or just look at the number nine.
As my pencil moves in such ways,
there's a slow that moves along with it.
But pay no attention to the mistake
you make.
There's this art I sold.
Just like it was gold.

> — *Tony, 15*
> *The Village School, Orlando*

Twelve

Experiment on things.
Go shopping.
Go to dances.
Meet friends.
Talk on the phone with your boyfriend.

> — *Shadrina, 12*
> *Capital City Youth Services, Tallahassee*

Seventeen

On the 17th of September,
I was born,
and ever since I can remember,
it has been my favorite number.
Maybe it's because it's the date of my birthday

— Or maybe not.

— Brenda, 16
PACE Center for Girls, Jacksonville

Eighteen

Such a realistic number I am.
How much abuse can this number withstand?
Responsibility, work, car, job, maybe even college,
TO GET A LITTLE KNOWLEDGE.
Ahhh, eighteen, prime, ready, and wanted,
unlike seventeen, when I was still taunted.
Eighteen: late nights, experience and love,
fully prominent, bringing ideas to the world above.
Nineteen can wait, even though it's around the corner,
but right now eighteen is still on my order.

— Frantz, 18
Miami Bridge Central

Twenty-Three

23 is the number of the day I was born.
Since that day, I have never been to a foreign country.
23 comes twelve times yearly,
and it's just that way.
'Cause only once a year it's my birthday.

— *Rose, 15*
PACE Center for Girls, Jacksonville

Twenty-Five

25 is silent,
although it could be very vibrant.
25 likes to be alone,
like a dog likes to fetch a bone.
It's usually at the end of a month,
when traffic is bunched.
It also stands for Christmas Day,
when all the kids love to play.

— *Monica, 16*
PACE Center for Girls, Jacksonville

Twenty-Eight

Dedicated to Laurie Spicer

Twenty-Eight represents
two 28th of Septembers:

First, happiness for a couple
starting a life together.

That has a chance to last.

Then, sadness.
While at another place,
not too far away,
someone takes her own life.

That's over too fast.

> *— Hope, 17*
> *PACE Center for Girls, Jacksonville*

Fifty

Does Fifty mean you're old?
Over the Hill?
Does Fifty mean wrinkles?
Grey Hair?
Does Fifty mean life's over,
Or just half started?

> *— Brooke, 18*
> *PACE Center for Girls, Jacksonville*

Steps

In Room 1001G,
brains click and rattle,
they work to the slow ticking of
the second hand.
They swallow, digest, and regurgitate
information on the pages of
blue lined paper.

In Room 1001G,
lips are smiling again
smiling at assignments completed
and grades received,
moving closer to the ultimate achievement
of self-worth.

— Tamara (Staff)
PACE Center for Girls, Jacksonville

The Lottery

If I won the Lottery,
I'd buy two Mercedes Benz,
two BMWs, and 16,000 beepers.

— Brian, 14
Capital City Youth Services, Tallahassee

X. Hopes, Dreams, and Fears

Contexts:

We work with many who are clinically depressed, who have turned their backs on the world or the adults in it, who are unable to lift a finger to help themselves, but we have also encountered a great deal of resiliency in unexpected faces. We offer them a chance to verbalize, to take into account and share the lessons of personal experience, to become more aware of social injustices and rewards, and to plan for better futures. Many of those who write with us readily acknowledge weaknesses and fears, but they also admit to hope and a deep desire for change. They testify not only to what is, but what could be, and by listening, we learn how to address their pain.

Anecdotes:

Antonio told us when we met him that he intended to become a DJ when he grew up. His skill with the microphone, his sense of timing and velvety voice suggested promise, and we grew to depend on him as a productive and talented contributor to our workshop. Our trust in him, however, was not fully founded, and on some days when we worked with him, Antonio was evasive and brooding, unable or unwilling to perform the simplest tasks. We learned from his poetry that his family was still a source of emotional turmoil, making him unpredictable and potentially disruptive in workshops. We began to worry about our upcoming performance and wondered if we had made a mistake in giving Antonio an important role. When it came time for him to perform, however, he found the reserves to make it work. Resisting what must have been a powerful urge to thwart the proceedings, he read his own poem about family violence and led others in a powerful recitation of Langston Hughes's "Brass Spittoons." For a moment, we all knew what it was like to succeed.

Sample Exercise:

*Write a poem about a time you were afraid or about a time when you **should have been** afraid but were not.*

I Fear Closeness

I fear my closeness
        to anyone I know,
for I am confused
        from head to toe.

Shakiness inside,
        trembling with fear,
afraid of being prosecuted
        by my peers.

Not knowing who's coming,
        left or right,
I feel like the devil's play toy
        in the middle of the night.

Blood rushes through my veins
        as it starts to boil.
Can't go to my mother, father,
        sister, or brother.

I deal with it on my own,
        but it still hurts inside.
Yet I must keep going
        from stride to stride.

—Antonio, 16
The Village School, Orlando

Judgement

Mom always said don't judge a book
by its cover,
but people often do,
such as
             all punks use drugs,
             all blacks are thieves,
             all Spanish are trouble.

When will all these untruths stop,
and who will stop them?
Someone put a foot down
        and put a different cover
           ON HUMAN LIFE,
        one that's all the same color.

                   — *Star, 17*
                   PACE Center for Girls, Orlando

Dreams

Love, War, and Hate are all a part of life.
Sometimes life just isn't fair. . .
One thing you may wish for is one day
a beautiful goddess will appear and grant
you three wishes. But in your mind you know
it is only a dream.

You know how wonderful a dream may be.
Just remember that dreaming, wishing,
is the most wonderful and healthy part of life.
Don't ever give up on your dreams.

— *Sandra, 16*
PACE Center for Girls, Orlando

Dreaming of Paradise

I dreamed
I was in Paradise
and not in this shelter,
and I would have
beautiful women
serving me, entertaining me,
and making my paradise
a fantastic, relaxing place.
Everytime I sleep,
I dream of
more magical paradise islands and worlds.

— *Bill, 13*
Capital City Youth Services

My Wish

I had a dream that I would
get rollerskates and rollerskate
in the Olympics. So for my birthday,
I made a wish, blew out my candles,
and my wish came true.

— Kaila, 16
PACE Center for Girls, Orlando

Beautiful Day

On an exciting, summer Saturday,
the flowers have bloomed,
the sky is blue, joyful children
are out playing softball.
The grass is green; the sun is shining
bright orange and yellow
— very nice, but hot. People
are at the beach, either
swimming or tanning.

— Beverly, 15
Family Services Program, Orlando

Summer

It was a beautiful, warm
summer day at the beach.
The sun was shining brightly,
the birds were flying,
people swimming in the blue
green ocean. Others were lying in the sun,
or building a sandcastle.

It was a great day!

— Brenda, 16
PACE Center for Girls, Jacksonville

Plant Life

Tall,
green,
yellow,
spiraling up,
cascading down.

Green and yellow,
variegated by God himself,
unique. . .
Like God
and
You and Me.

Struggling for the light,
as man struggles
through life.
Leaves pointing up,
leaves pointing down.

Joy,
depression,
young leaves,
old leaves,
dead leaves.

> — *Lamar (Staff)*
> *Interface, Gainesville*

Storm

It was a muggy Sunday night,
when voices started to rumble.
Objects were being thrown,
but the noise didn't seem
to matter anymore.
All the lights were out,
the wind started to howl.
Buildings started to fall.
Just as quick as the blink of an eye,
thousands of people in a town
were totally wiped out.
As the wind and storm died down,
everything was over.
These were days of fear.

> — *Sandra, 16*
> *PACE Center for Girls, Orlando*

Steel and Sky

Power lines, steel webs confine,
violating the brownish sky.
Hard gray smothers earthlike cancer.
Cracks revealing ground below.
Broken and bleeding,
every seed, every stone.

— Gen, 16
PACE Center for Girls, Orlando

Seeing this Needle

Well, there was a time
when I was pregnant,
and my water broke.
I was rushed to the hospital.
There, I was having contractions.
Then they started numbing me up,
and I remember seeing this needle
almost the size of a ruler
about to stick me in my stomach.
I always had this fear of hospitals.
I felt like I would die in a hospital.

— Mevonda, 16
PACE Center for Girls, Orlando

Marigold

There once was a place I did not know of,
a place with lots of silence.

There once was a place where people shout,
a place where everybody's heart is full of marigold,
a place full of all different collections
of birds and gold.

A place where no one's been before.
A place where there is peace.

A place where you go when you are six feet deep.

               — Angela, 12
                    Capital City Youth Services, Tallahassee

Pregnant

Being pregnant is the most
fearful and afraid thing.

You'll have contractions
and pains.

Pregnant can cause death
to most people who have
mental problems.

And I remember that day
I went into the delivery room.

But things just didn't
come out right.

— Marsha, 15
Capital City Youth Services, Tallahassee

Innocence Lost

The sun shines bright on this beautiful day,
with children running free and laughter sounding.
The last of the innocent
and the ones who will fight to keep them that way.
For in the world today, with the wars and the violence,
there isn't very much innocence left.

> — *Kimber, 15*
> *PACE Center for Girls, Tallahassee*

I Wish I Could Eat and Sleep Forever

I wish I could eat and sleep forever.
When I get home,
I am going to catch me some zzzzzz.
I am going to sleep for everybody in the world
and eat the whole weekend.
I wish I owned Magic Waterbed and Albertson's.

> — *Danielle, 18*
> *PACE Center for Girls, Orlando*

Not going forward

not being able to move,
a huge abyss, darkness, nothing:
no thoughts,
no talk,
no friends,
no dreams,
no goals,
no going forward.
Stagnation,
endless time,
tedious monotony.
Boredom.

— Michelle (Staff)
PACE Center for Girls, Orlando

As I Watch

As I watch a little boy
shy from a woman who gives warmth,
I watch with sorrow
in my eyes.

As I watch a woman
spill the blood of another,
I cry.

As I watch the boy try
but never succeed
to flee from his monster,
I watch with fright.

As I watch from a window,
a little boy fails to fight back
and dies.

As I watch with sad eyes,
I turn from this window
to forget what has happened.

— Cathy, 15
PACE Center for Girls, Orlando

Someone is Coming

Someone is coming.
Someone is near.
But seeing no one, I am in fear.
But it is just my shadow
who is constantly there.
Wherever I go,
he is there.
Whatever I do,
he is scared.
But he's still there.
When we hear screams,
we start to run.
When I turn a corner,
he is gone.
But when I hit a light,
but not bright,
he is there,
but in fright.

> — *Shawn, 17*
> *YouthBuild, Tallahassee*

XI. Love

Contexts:

We try not to give assignments on love, hoping to avoid the generic responses that such invitations yield, but we do find love in the poems written in these workshops, sneaking in between the lines, asking to be acknowledged or understood. Writers generally find ways of including their obsessions in their work, whether they write from the shelter, the suburbs, or from urban coffee shops. If love is their obsession (as often it is), indirection may lend uniqueness to what they say. Poetry is therapy insomuch as it puts us in touch with who we are and what we desire. Manipulating language, making verbal and technical decisions, we give shape to experience, convincing ourselves in the process of our own universality. To push through difficulty is itself an act of love and a testament to our obsession.

Anecdotes:

Jill claimed that she had everything she could want in her boyfriend. When they were together, it didn't matter where they were or what they did. She didn't have to write the assignment the way we had asked her, since she felt the difficulty was pointless in her condition of perfect, accomplished love. She told me she was waiting for him to get out of prison and for her to turn 18, so that they could start their life together, independent of present troubles. This was her hope and, to her mind, the answer to her pain. The necessity of seeking out new language for this emotion was a distraction from her purpose and a possible jinx on her plans. She didn't feel we were sensitive or wise because we tried to make her see it another way.

Sample Exercise:

For Valentine's Day, write or imagine a beautiful scene that expresses the way you feel about the person you love. Do not mention the word "love" directly in the poem, but try to convey the intensity of your emotion through the scene itself.

Baby, Baby, Baby

Crying through the night,
never asleep.
Crying all night.
Crying upon sunset.
Little baby, oh baby,
my sweet little baby,
please stay quiet
until the sunrise.

— Sabrina,
PACE Center for Girls, Jacksonville

Caution: Police Line; Do Not Cross

Someone lies dead and gone,
all because of a jealous rage.

She thought she was safe from him.
She thought she had escaped all the domestic abuse.

He came in with a long sharp knife,
All because she was his wife.

— Tasha, 16
PACE Center for Girls, Tallahassee

Your Eyes are Blue

Your eyes are blue
like the sky.
Your shoes are black.
Your dress is red
like the ribbon
on my poetry book for AIDS.

— *Black X, 17*
Miami Bridge, Homestead

The Prettiest Girl

It looks like she likes the color red.
When she smiles,
I like to smile back.
The way she acts is the most.
I like her with this green blouse,
with her hair tossed back.
Her hair is the prettiest I have
ever seen.

— *Bill, 12*
Interface, Gainesville

Love

A love is not a love.
Love is power.
But my love for you
is superlove.

—Jimmy, 13
Family Services Program, Orlando

I Picture You and Me Walking

I picture you and me walking
down the beach as the sun sets.
Then you stop and take me in your arms,
ever so gently and kiss me, ever so lightly,
caressing me, then I say, "Stop!"

— Candace, 12
Arnette House, Ocala

My Girl

Me and my workers went to the beach.
We saw a lady who looked lovely in peach.
It was hot, and the sun was out.
She was coming out of the water,
and I began to shout.
She turned and looked and began to fall,
so I swept her up, and we went to the Mall.

— *Denham, 18*
YouthBuild, Tallahassee

It was a Bright and Sunny Day

It was a bright and sunny day.
All the kids were already out to play.
In the distance, you could hear the chirping of birds.
In the kitchen, my mom sang a song with beautiful words.

I got up and went to the mall,
where everybody was having a ball.
I bought my girlfriend an engagement ring,
knowing that soon I'll be her king.

— *Karl (Staff)*
Family Services Program, Orlando

Sometimes I Wonder

Sometimes I wonder,
how long will I wait,
how long will I go on anticipating,
how long will I have to endure the pain,

seeing you laughing without me in your life,
holding onto the ever-so-short memories?
Wanting to hold you and knowing I can't
cuts across my heart like a knife.

Someday I will walk hand in hand with you,
and I will be what you want in your life.
That's why I say, "Please don't give up on love!"
because I want to go on in life with you,
being there for you,
through thick and thin,
until the end.

— *Regina, 16*
YouthBuild, Tallahassee

What Is Love

"What is love?"
"Will I ever be loved?"
I ask my parents.
They say it's just when two people
love each other.
So, then I say, "Will I ever be loved?"
"I don't know," they say.
So, now, I'm asking you,
"Will I ever be loved?"

— *Amanda, 13*
Capital City Youth Services, Tallahassee

When You Are Here

I laugh
I smile
I feel warm, safe, and special.
I feel loved, beautiful.
I also feel like the most special girl in the world.

But, now, you are gone, and I am sad.
I cry.
I feel cold, unsafe, unwanted.
I feel unloved, ugly.

I don't know what love is, so
I ask, "What is love?"

— *Amanda, 13*
Capital City Youth Services, Tallahassee

Abandonment

There's nothing I won't do
to try and turn your head around.
There's nothing I won't say
to get you to hear me.
Cheap words are spoken,
and they're flushed down a pipe drain.
They spin and they turn,
but they never go anywhere.
They only make me pace the floor,
chew my nails to the bone,
and wait for the fervid
words that I want to hear.

— *Tamara (Staff)*
PACE Center for Girls, Jacksonville

XII. Laughter

Contexts:

You would expect from the backgrounds and current situations of these young people that humor would have little to do with their lives, but many still appreciate laughter and have the verbal skills and intelligence to make it happen. They have used it, certainly, to get under the skin of counselors and teachers, or to undermine a system in which they are sometimes considered to be the lowest value. When they direct these instincts more positively, they show how generous they truly can be. We are often surprised at the humor generated in these workshops, the playfulness we uncover in these street-wise youths, and we do our best to please them back with our own brand of off-the-wall humor. In the end, laughter is the most reliable sign that trust has been established, that we are working together and finding ways of escaping the pain, if only for a short time.

Anecdotes:

Mevonda thought that we didn't realize what a good poet she was, how much she brought to the group in terms of energy and entertainment. While we tried to express our appreciation of her work, she remained somewhat cool in her reception, reluctant to give her approval until she could be sure we were okay. At one of our workshops, we played a recording of June Jordan's "Menu," a repetition poem in which Jordan lists all of the kinds of chicken one might or might not find on a menu. Mevonda wrote "Choke Nuts" in response, and everyone laughed when she read it, pleased and surprised by its potentially off-color allusions. Much to Mevonda's credit, "Choke Nuts" continues to be a favorite with other workshops. When participants read sample poems, everyone wants to know more about "Choke Nuts" and the person who wrote it. I tell them about the sixteen-year-old mother with a cast on her leg who responded with imagination and ease to the writing assignments. She was working then on her high school diploma. She graduated from PACE Center for Girls, Orlando, in June 1993.

Sample Exercise:

Write a list poem, beginning every line with "We've got..." and ending each line with some silly or colorful variation on what you've got on your list to sell or eat or keep. June Jordan's "Menu" or Mevonda's "Choke Nuts" may be used as an example of how this kind of poem is done.

Choke Nuts

I got me some choke nuts.
I got some coffee nuts.
I got some pork and beans nuts.
I got some peel your toe nail nuts.
Then I have more choke nuts.
I had some crusty frog nuts.
I had some squished roach nuts.
I had some vitamin nuts.
I had some burnt tire nuts.
I had some beach nuts.
I had even more choke nuts.
I had some canon ball nuts.
I had some hairy crusty nuts.
I had some toe jam nuts.
I got choked on those choke nuts.

— Mevonda, 16
PACE Center for Girls, Orlando

Uncontrollable Mascara

There once was a rat
who had uncontrollable mascara.
The rat was personally forced to tame
his mascara constantly.
He then resolved the problem
by flattening the poor mascara.

—Joy, 15
PACE Center for Girls, Orlando

Hijacked

One day my plane got,
hijacked, and the man
was fashionably dressed,
but quite sweaty.

— Heather, 16
PACE Center for Girls, Orlando

The Snoring Fisher

Tom went on a fishing trip last night.
He had to drive 100 miles to get there.
On the way, he took a break
and fell asleep. Tom snored so loud,
he woke himself up.
After that, he went on his way.

> *— Angela, 16*
> *PACE Center for Girls, Orlando*

The Taste of Laughter

If laughter had a taste,
which I could hardly imagine,
it's probably taste
like strawberry or cherries.

> *— Sylvia, 17*
> *PACE Center for Girls, Tallahassee*

Fried Roaches

We have flattened roaches.
We have rush-to-the-hospital roaches.
We have slippery roaches.
We have eggshell roaches.

But we ain't got no fried roaches.

We have high-heel roaches.
We have orbit roaches.
We have dream-bow roaches.

But we ain't got no fried roaches.

We got mailbox roaches.
We got fly away roaches.
We got tic-tac-toe roaches.
We got rollerskating roaches.

But...Oops...We got one fried roach.

— Mevonda, 16
PACE Center for Girls, Orlando

The Taste of Laughter

If laughter had a taste
it would taste like
a really sour lemon
and some fizz that tickles
when it gets in your mouth.

> — *Sheree, 16*
> *PACE Center for Girls, Tallahassee*

Cake

We have pull-a-piece of cake.
We have fashionable cake.
We have snazzy cake.

But we ain't got no dog chocolate cake.

I was fashionable gettin my cake.
Snazzy as the cake was, it could win 1st place.
I pulled that sucker out and dug in and ate it.

But we ain't got no horse chocolate cake.

The cake was pulled apart.
Roach fashionable was not the style.
Snazzy is the safest way
to eat it.

But they ain't got my favorite cake:
doo brown cake.

> — *Tiffany, 16*
> *PACE Center for Girls, Orlando*

Bubba I

Me and my baby Bubba
robbed an earring store
in the middle of the day
and got away.

Bubba II

The image of a fine strong black man
is encouraging while walking
your ass to school,
but there is a scary sight:
a white boy trying to talk to ya.
As I take a drag of my Newport,
I ask the brother man if
he wants one.
Of course, he says yes.
Then the white boy, he says,
"No way, I'm a Marlboro Man."

Well, this is the end of my creative poem.
"Whoa," says the crowd.

— *Erica, 17*
PACE Center for Girls, Orlando

Index

A

B

C

D

Daphne (Staff), Youth & Family Connection South, St.Petersburg 23, 52, 67
Dee, 16, Capital City Youth Services 5, 12, 22, 31, 47
Denham, 18, YouthBuild, Tallahassee 17, 107
Derrick, 18 YouthBuild, Tallahassee 29
Diana, 14, Haven Poe Runaway Center, Tampa 19, 43

E

Eleina,16, PACE Center for Girls, Orlando 50, 55
Elmer, 14, Youth Crisis Center North, Jacksonville 17, 70
Elmer, 14, Youth Crisis Center South, Jacksonville 42
Erica, 17, PACE Center for Girls, Orlando 117
Evelin, 18, Arnette House, Ocala 40

F

Fat Rat, 13, Miami Bridge, Homestead 17, 45
Frantz, 18, Miami Bridge Central 4, 44, 82

G

Gen, 16, PACE Center for Girls, Orlando 95
Ginger, 18, YouthBuild, Tallahassee 25

H

Heather, 16, PACE Center for Girls, Orlando 113
Heather, 16, PACE Center for Girls, Jacksonville 8
Hope, 17, PACE Center for Girls, Jacksonville 84

J

James, 12, Arnette House, Ocala 10
James, 15 — 19
Jeanette, 14 — 23
Jennifer, 17, PACE Center for Girls, Tallahassee 34
Jennifer,15, Haven Poe Runaway Center, Tampa 19, 42
Jessica, 11, Capital City Youth Services, Tallahassee 66
Jimmy, 13, Family Services Program, Orlando 60, 106
John, 17, YouthBuild, Tallahassee, 36
Joseph, 14, Family Services Program, Orlando 59
Joy, 15, PACE Center for Girls, Orlando 113
Julette (Staff), Family Services Program, Orlando 61
Julia, 12, Capital City Youth Services, Tallahassee 45
Juliee, 16 — 17

K

K.K.R, 15, Haven Poe Runaway Center, Tampa 43
Kaila, 16, PACE Center for Girls, Orlando 31, 51, 91
Karen (Staff), BEACH House, Daytona Beach 35
Karl (Staff), Family Services Program, Orlando 61, 107
Kellie, PACE Center for Girls, Tallahassee 20
Keyshonda, PACE Center for Girls, Tallahassee 20, 30
Kim, PACE Center for Girls, Tallahassee 20
Kimber, 15, PACE Center for Girls, Tallahassee 20, 30, 44, 98
Kurtis, 17, YouthBuild, Tallahassee 25

L

La Tasha, 13, Capital City Youth Services, Tallahassee 50
Lakena, 15, PACE Center for Girls, Orlando 60
Lakesha, 17, YouthBuild, Tallahassee 25
Lamar (Staff), Interface, Gainesville 93
Lamont, 20, YouthBuild, Tallahassee 34
Latoya, 17, YouthBuild, Tallahassee 25, 54
Lisa, 16, The Village School, Orlando 53

M

Marcell, 18, YouthBuild, Tallahassee 25
Marsha, 15, Capital City Youth Services, Tallahassee 97
Melissa, 13, BEACH House, Daytona Beach 29
Mevonda, PACE Center for Girls, Orlando 7, 95, 112, 115
Michelle (Staff), PACE Center for Girls, Orlando 99
Monica, 16, PACE Center for Girls, Jacksonville 83

N

Nate, 16, YouthBuild, Tallahassee 25

P

Pam, 17, PACE Center for Girls, Tallahassee 51
Paul, 14, Youth & Family Connection North, Clearwater 13, 23, 53
Paula, 16, PACE Center for Girls, Orlando 64

R

Rachel, 16, PACE Center for Girls, Orlando 33
Regina, 16, YouthBuild, Tallahassee 108
Roderick, 18, YouthBuild, Tallahassee 25

Ronald, 16, Family Services Program, Orlando 59
Rose, 15, PACE Center for Girls, Jacksonville 83

S

T

Recent Books from Anhinga Press

Walking Back to Woodstock
Earl S. Braggs, 1996

Hello Stranger: Beach Poems
Robert Dana, 1996

Isle of Flowers: Poems by Florida's Individual Artist Fellows
Donna J. Long, Helen Pruitt Wallace, Rick Campbell, eds., 1995

Unspeakable Strangers:
Descents into the Dark Self, Ascent into the Light
Van K. Brock, 1995

The Secret Life of Moles
P.V. LeForge, 1992

Random Descent
Gary Corseri, 1988

North of Wakulla: An Anthology
M. J. Ryals and D. Decker, eds.,1988

The Anhinga Prize for Poetry Series

Man Under a Pear Tree
Keith Ratzlaff, 1996

Easter Vigil
Ann Neelon, 1995

Mass For The Grace of A Happy Death
Frank X. Gaspar, 1994

The Physicist At The Mall
Janet Holmes, 1993

Hat Dancer Blue
Earl S. Braggs, 1992

Hands
Jean Monahan, 1991